What Is A Rocket

By Theodore W. Munch, Ed. D.

Professor of Science Education   University of Arizona

Pictures — Berthold Tiedemann

BENEFIC PRESS · CHICAGO

Publishing Division of Beckley-Cardy Company

Atlanta 3, Georgia   Dallas 1, Texas
Long Beach 3, California   Portland 4, Oregon

The WHAT IS IT Series

What Is A Plant

What Is A Season

What Is A Turtle

What Is A Bird

What Is A Chicken

What Is A Fish

What Is A Butterfly

What Is A Cow

What Is A Frog

What Is A Tree

What Is A Rock

What Is A Magnet

What Is A Rocket

What Is A Solar System

What Is A Machine

What Is Light

What Is Air

What Is Gravity

What Is Weather

What Is Electricity

What Is Water

What Is Sound

What Is A Star

Library of Congress
Number 59-12333

CONTENTS

THIS IS A ROCKET

A rocket is a simple engine.

It may be small like the rocket on this page or big like the rocket on page four.

The rocket is the simplest kind of engine because it has only two main parts. A simple rocket engine has no moving parts.

You can see the two parts of the
rocket engine on the rocket shown
here. The first part is the tube.
The fuel is inside the tube.

The other part of the rocket engine
is the hole where the gases from the
burning fuel pass out. This hole is
the nozzle.

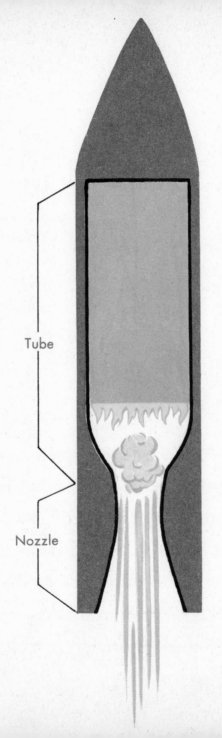

Tube

Nozzle

7

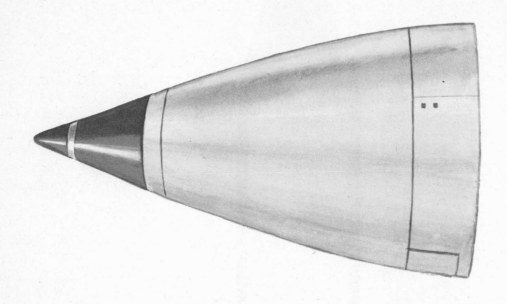

At the end of the rocket tube is a
pointed cone. This cone makes the
front end or nose of the rocket sharp.
The sharp, pointed nose of the rocket
can cut through the air better than
a flat nose can. This helps the
rocket to fly faster.

WHAT MAKES A ROCKET MOVE

The force which moves a rocket works on the action-reaction idea. You can see action and reaction at work around you all the time.

It can be seen when a swimmer dives off a raft into the water. When the swimmer dives, he goes one way. This is the action. The raft goes the opposite way. This is the reaction.

When the swimmer dived into the water his legs pushed him up and out. The pushing of his legs was the action.

But something besides the swimmer moved. The action of his legs also pushed the raft. The raft went the other way. The moving of the raft was the reaction.

Another way to show the
action-reaction idea
is by using a toy balloon.

If air is forced into a balloon, it is squeezed into a
small space. When air or gas is squeezed into a small
space, it pushes on the sides of whatever is holding it.

When the stem of the
balloon is held closed,
the air inside pushes against
the sides of the balloon.

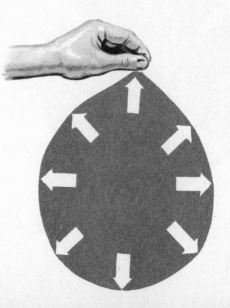

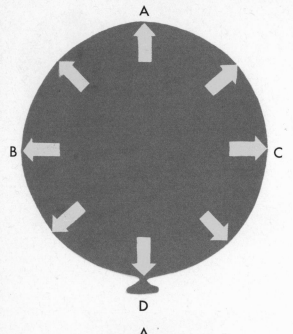

It is important to remember that the air inside the balloon is pushing against each side with the same amount of force. The air pressure is equal on all sides of the balloon.

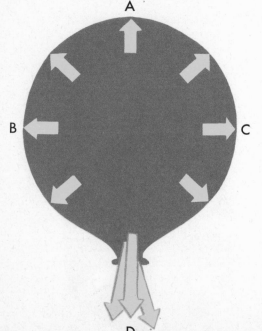

When the balloon is released, the stem opens. Some of the air that was pushing against side D rushes out. Now there is less air pressure on side D than on the other three sides.

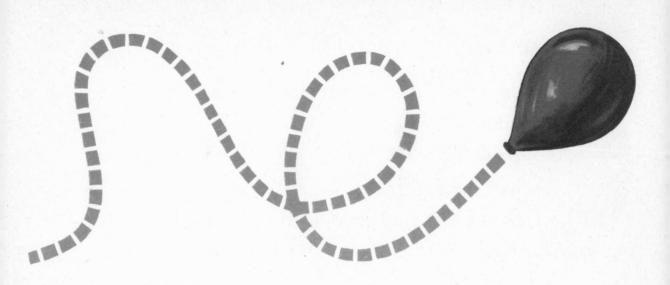

The air inside the balloon cannot push on the sides with the same amount of pressure. There is less air pressure on one side than on the other three sides. The sides are no longer balanced.

The air is pushing harder on side A than on side D because there is more air on side A. The harder push on side A makes the balloon move in that direction.

The air rushing out of one side is the action.

The moving of the balloon in the opposite direction is the reaction.

Now let us see the action and reaction in a simple type of rocket.

The rocket goes into the air when the fuel is set on fire. When the fuel burns, gases are formed inside the tube. These gases push against the sides of the tube just as the air pushes against the sides of the balloon. The gases near the nozzle rush out.

Just as in the balloon, the push of the gases in the end of the tube is less than at the front. The rocket is pushed forward by gases nearest the nose.

The rushing of the gases out the tail of the rocket is the action. The moving of the rocket in the opposite direction is the reaction. The rocket will keep going until all the fuel is burned.

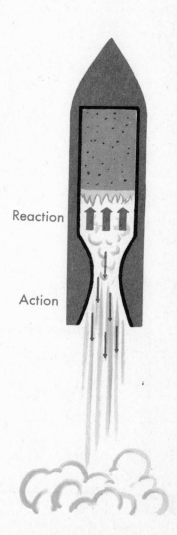

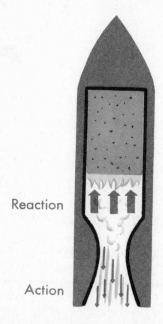

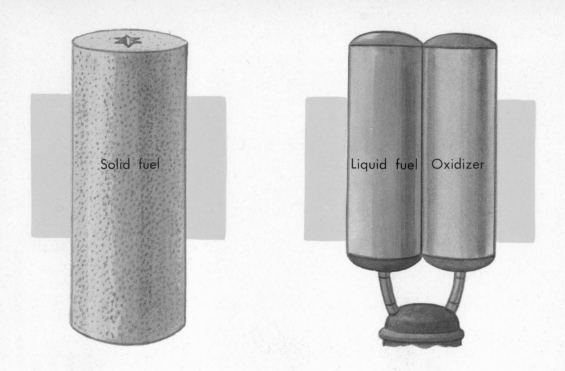

Solid fuel

Liquid fuel Oxidizer

FUEL FOR THE ROCKET

The fuel for the simple rocket on pages 14 and 15 is solid fuel. Solid fuel for a rocket comes in a roll or cake which is burned inside the rocket tube.

Some rockets use fuel that is in liquid form.

Some of the new liquid fuels do not have to be set on fire. When these fuels are mixed, they form gases which push the rocket forward.

A fuel must have oxygen to burn in a rocket engine. When fuels burn on earth, they use the oxygen of the air. Many rockets go high above the earth where there is not enough oxygen to burn the rocket fuel. Rockets must take their own supply of oxygen with them in the form of a chemical. This chemical is called the oxidizer. Oxidizers are used in both solid and liquid rocket fuels.

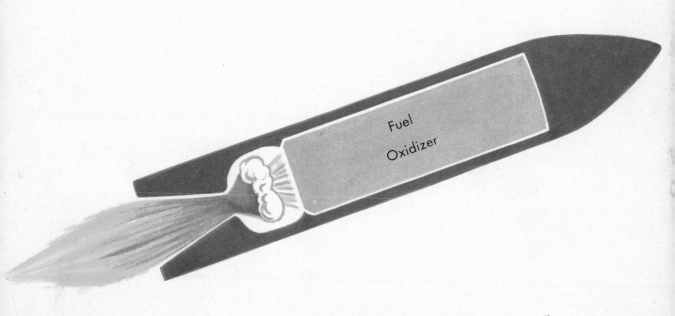

Some of the newest solid fuels are made by mixing the fuel and oxidizer with a rubber-like plastic. This mixture is then poured into the rocket tube where it hardens. A hole remains in the center of the cake of solid fuel to help it burn evenly.

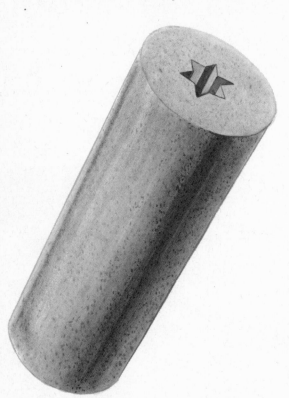

Rocket men have found that a star-shaped hole is one of the best.

The fuel begins to burn when it is set on fire by a type of spark plug. The burning of the fuel may also be started by exploding a small powder charge.

The fuel burns outward from the hole. The hot gases which are formed rush out of the nozzle.

Most of the first rockets that were built used solid
fuel. The solid-fuel rockets were easy to make, but the
fuel did not always burn evenly. This made the gas
pressure uneven inside the tube. The rocket would twist
and turn instead of flying straight. The new solid fuels
do not do this. They burn evenly.

Solid fuels can be stored for a long time. They are
also safer to handle than liquid fuels. In the future,
more rockets will use better solid fuels.

The solid-fuel rockets shown on this page are being
stored under the ground.

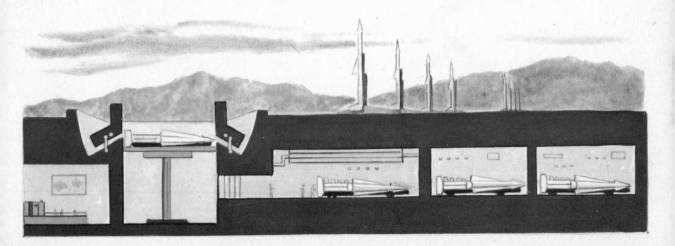

Rocket men have worked to find liquid fuels to use in rockets, also. There are some important kinds of rockets that burn liquid fuels.

Liquid-fuel rockets are not as simple to make as solid-fuel rockets because they have more parts.

In a liquid-fuel rocket, there are two separate tanks. One tank is for the fuel, and the other is for the oxidizer.

There is a separate firing chamber where the fuel is burned.

There is a pump to force the fuel and oxidizer through the pipes and into the firing chamber. The nozzle is at the other end of the chamber.

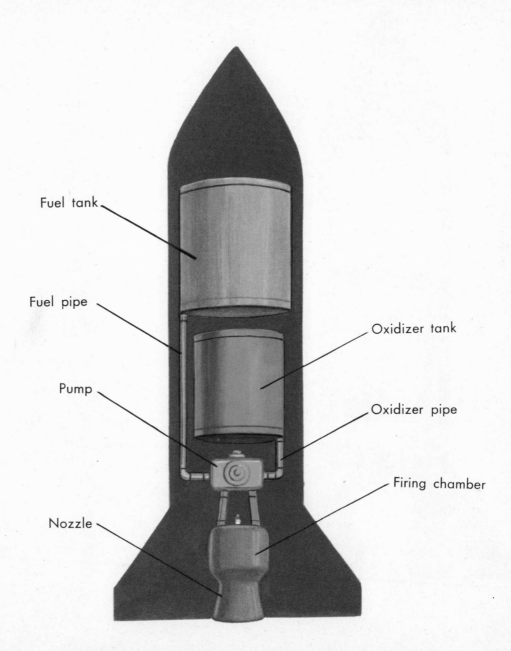

Fuel tank

Fuel pipe

Pump

Nozzle

Oxidizer tank

Oxidizer pipe

Firing chamber

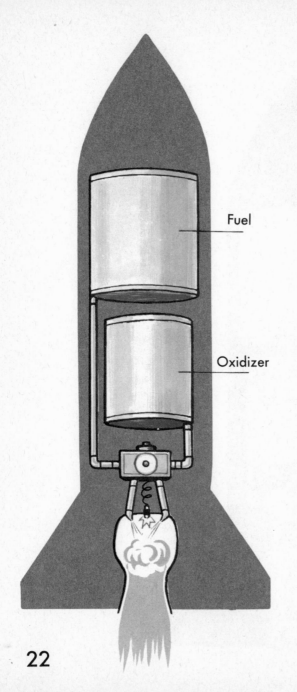

Fuel

Oxidizer

When the fuel and the oxidizer meet in the firing chamber, they start to burn. In many cases, the fuel and the oxidizer do not need a spark to start them burning. They form hot gases just by coming together.

Some of the gases rush out the nozzle. The rest of the gases stay in the firing chamber and push the rocket in the opposite direction.

The action-reaction idea is working here, too.

There is one more thing
that some liquid-fuel rockets
have. They have a way of
cooling the walls of the
rocket engine. The burning
fuel makes enough heat to
burn through the walls of
the rocket engine.

One important way to
keep the rocket engine cool
is to run coils of pipe around the firing chamber.
A cold liquid is pumped through these pipes. This
keeps the firing chamber cool.

Some rockets use both liquid and solid fuels.
The rockets used to send satellites far into space
carry tanks of liquid fuel and cakes of solid fuel.
The liquid fuel is fired first, and the solid fuel is
burned later on. Some rockets burn 1000 pounds
of liquid fuel each second.

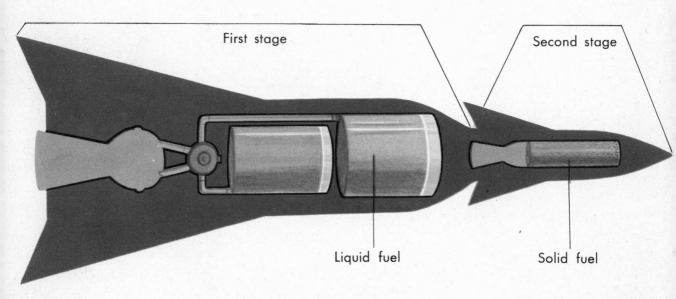

First stage

Second stage

Liquid fuel

Solid fuel

When it is time to fire the rocket, the rocket men go into a small control house with thick walls. The thick walls protect the men from the heat and gases that come from the rocket.

To fire the rocket, the men push an electric switch inside the control house. Electricity flows through a wire to inside the rocket. The fuel begins to burn, and the rocket begins its journey.

FLYING STRAIGHT WITH A SPACE ROCKET

Men knew how to make simple rockets a long time ago, but they did not use them very much. They did not know how to control the rockets.

Rocket men today are working hard to learn how to make a rocket fly straight and steady. One way to do this is to put fins or wings on a rocket.

Without fins the rocket might fly around like this.
It would not go the way the rocket men want it to go.
But with fins, the rocket will fly straight and steady.
If the rocket tries to turn, air pushing on the fins will
balance it again.

Some rockets have wings, fins, and a tailpiece, too.

These three parts help to guide the rocket as long as it is within the blanket of air around the earth. But once the rocket is high enough to leave this blanket of air, the wings, fins, and tailpiece are of no help. There is no air in space to push on these parts and steady the rocket. Rocket men must have other ways to guide the rocket at these heights.

Another way to make a rocket fly straight is to make it spin around and around very fast as it flies through the air. A spinning rocket can fly straight and smoothly.

Rocket men know several ways
to make a rocket spin.

The most common way is to put
several nozzles around the body
of the rocket.

The nozzles are placed
in such a way that the
streams of gas coming
out of the nozzles
will push at
an angle to
each other.

This makes the
rocket spin. The rocket
men can make the rocket
spin as fast or as slowly as
they want by placing the nozzles in
different positions and by making
the nozzles larger or smaller.

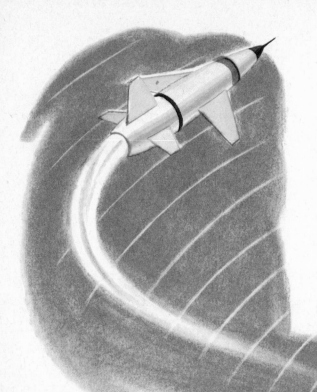

Some rockets can change
direction in flight.
Rocket men use radar
instruments to send radio
beams to the flying rocket.
Special controls on the
rocket receive the beams.
The controls then move
the fins or wings.

The levers on the rocket
make the fins or wings
move. This will change
the direction of the air
pressure on the parts.
The rocket will turn.

Rocket men can also make a rocket turn by changing the direction of the gases pouring out of the nozzle.

In a rocket of this type, the whole firing chamber is placed in a type of ring inside the tube. Radio beams sent to the rocket can make the firing chamber move. By moving the firing chamber, the direction of the gases coming from the nozzle is changed. The rocket will turn in the opposite direction from the gases. The action-reaction idea is at work here.

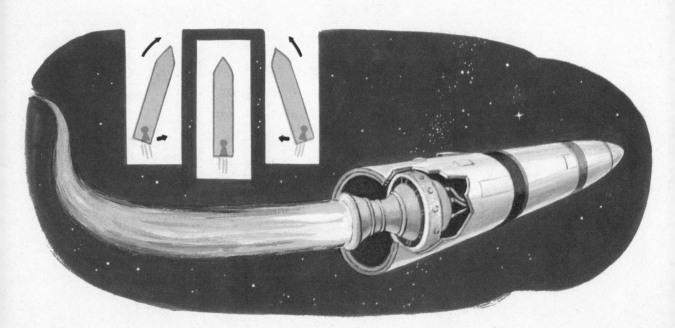

USES OF ROCKETS

There are many different kinds of rockets that have many different uses.

Rockets that go out into space can tell scientists many things. There are radio instruments inside the nose cones that send back to earth information about temperature, cloud formations, magnetic fields around the earth, and many other things.

Rockets have an important use in time of war. Explosives instead of instruments can be put in the nose cone. These explosives go off when the rocket hits its target. These rockets are called missiles.

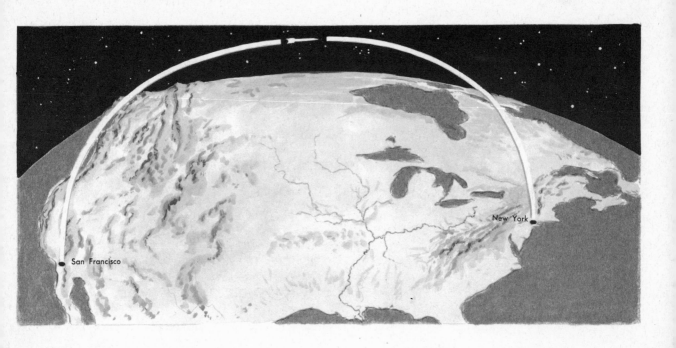

Rockets can be used to carry mail. The mail bags are put into the rocket, and are dropped by parachute over the place where the mail is to be delivered.

Mail could be sent from New York to California in just a few minutes by rocket.

There are some missiles that can be shot from a submarine underwater. The rocket engine starts to fire after the rocket is above the water.

Controls on the submarine guide the missile to its target. Some missiles of this type can be shot at targets more than a thousand miles away.

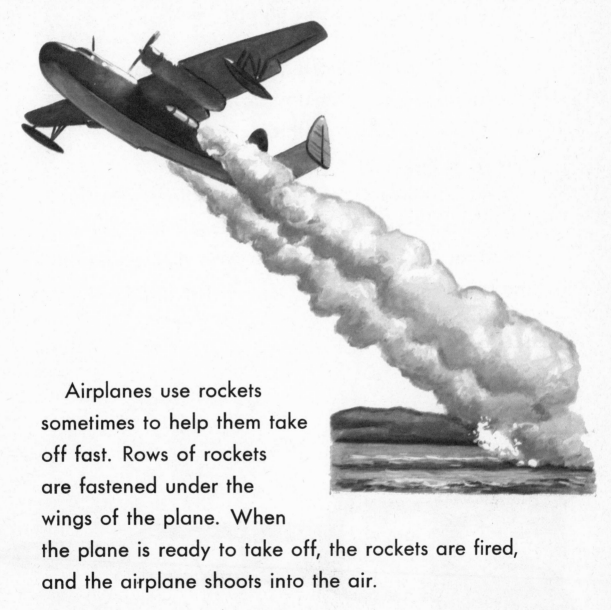

Airplanes use rockets
sometimes to help them take
off fast. Rows of rockets
are fastened under the
wings of the plane. When
the plane is ready to take off, the rockets are fired,
and the airplane shoots into the air.

ROCKETS IN SPACE

Rockets that are built to go a long way are called many-stage rockets. A many-stage rocket is really several rockets in one. A three-stage rocket, like this one, is three rockets put together.

There are three separate rocket engines. The third rocket is small and fits inside the nose cone of the second rocket. In rockets of this type, the second and third stages may use solid fuel and the first stage may use liquid fuel.

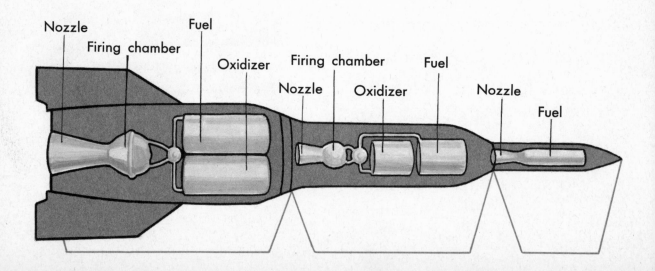

Nozzle   Fuel

Firing chamber

Oxidizer   Firing chamber   Fuel

Nozzle   Oxidizer   Nozzle

Fuel

When the first rocket in
the three-stage rocket has
used all its fuel, it falls away.
Then the second rocket
begins to fire. When its
fuel is gone, it, too, falls
away. The third rocket is
left to travel to the end of
the flight.

An artificial satellite may be
attached to the third rocket.
At just the right moment, the
satellite is released.

The satellite may circle
the earth for a long time.
It may carry radio instruments
to send messages to earth.

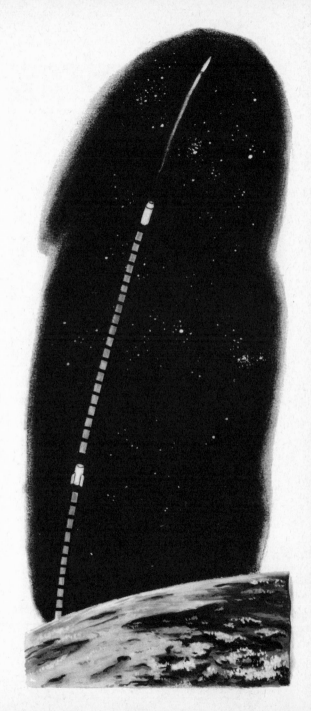

For a space rocket, the first part of the journey is the hardest. Before it can get into space, the rocket must move fast enough to break away from the pull of the earth's gravity. This speed is called escape velocity.

The escape velocity from earth is about seven miles per second. If the rocket cannot travel that fast, the gravity of the earth will pull it back.

Once the rocket has escaped the gravity of the earth, the journey becomes easier. If the rocket is going to the moon, for example, the gravity of the moon will pull it the rest of the way.

The gravity of the moon and the gravity of the earth are equal at a certain point. Anything placed on the earth side would be pulled toward the earth. Anything on the moon side would be pulled toward the moon.

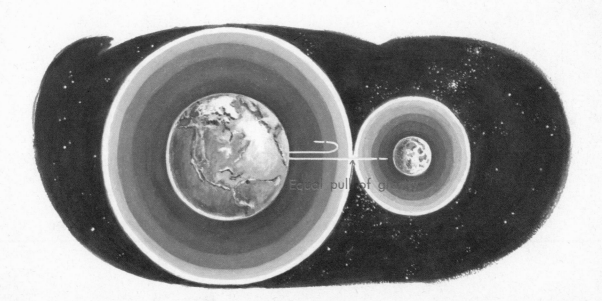

Equal pull of gravity

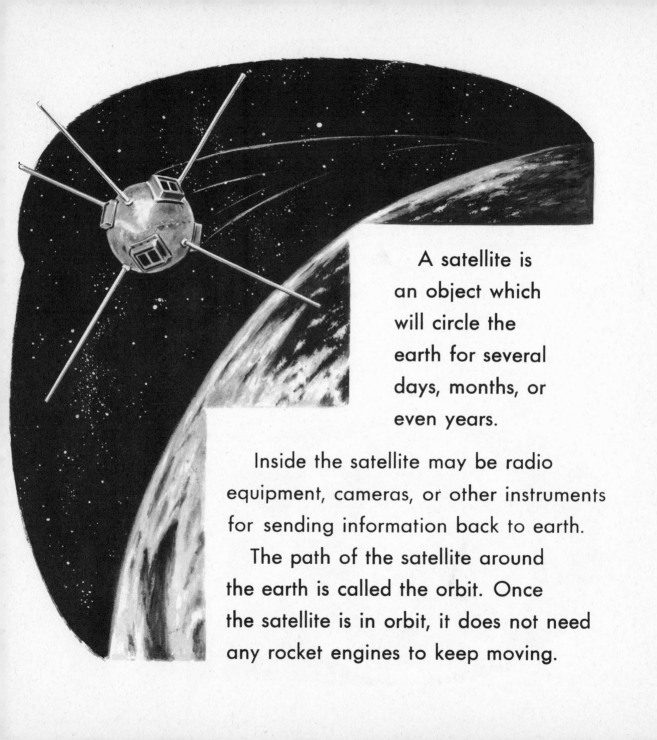

A satellite is
an object which
will circle the
earth for several
days, months, or
even years.

Inside the satellite may be radio
equipment, cameras, or other instruments
for sending information back to earth.
The path of the satellite around
the earth is called the orbit. Once
the satellite is in orbit, it does not need
any rocket engines to keep moving.

If the satellite is going at a speed just under escape velocity, it will go into orbit.

To see how this happens, we must first know this important rule of science:

Any moving object tends to travel in a straight line. The object will continue to travel until something stops it.

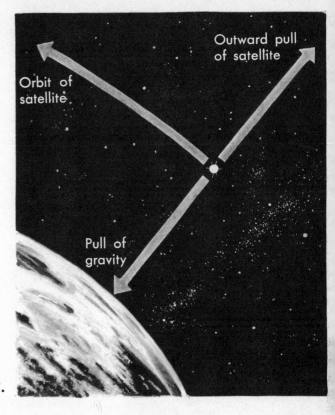

When a satellite is launched, it tends to travel in a straight line right out into space. But since it does not reach escape velocity, the satellite is pulled back by the gravity of the earth. When the pull of gravity and the outward pull of the moving satellite are equal, the satellite circles the earth in orbit.

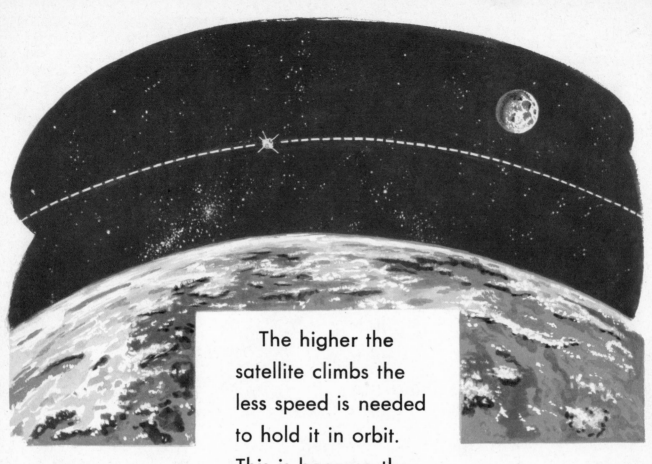

The higher the
satellite climbs the
less speed is needed
to hold it in orbit.
This is because the
pull of gravity grows smaller higher above the earth.
When the satellite is very high above the earth, it
needs less speed to balance the pull of gravity than
it would at a lesser height.

In time the satellite will lose speed and fall toward the earth. Even at great heights, there is enough air to cause friction and gradually slow down the satellite.

Nearer the earth, friction of the denser air will cause the satellite to burn up. Some rockets have special nose cones that will not burn. These nose cones come back to earth.

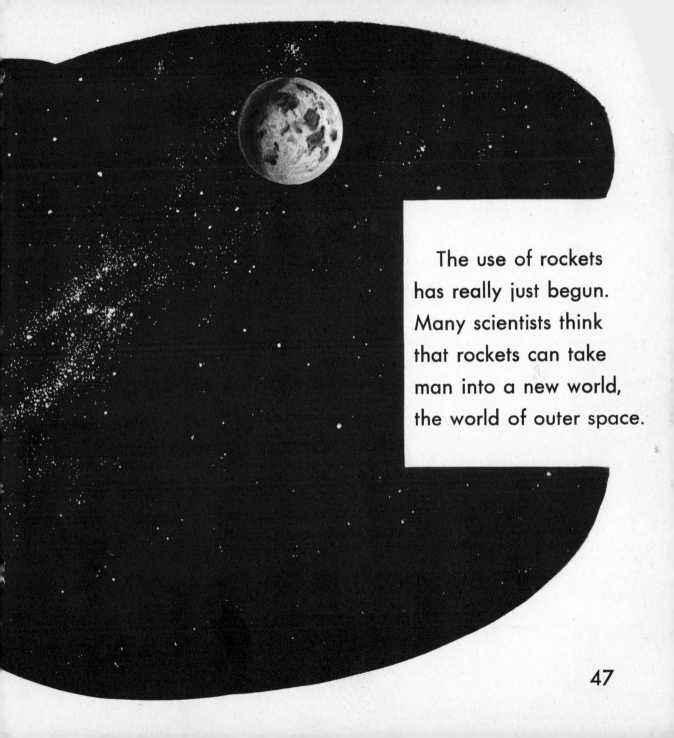

The use of rockets
has really just begun.
Many scientists think
that rockets can take
man into a new world,
the world of outer space.

47

PICTURE DICTIONARY

ACTION — The doing of something or the causing of something to move or to change. A boy jumping off a raft is an action. 5

FIRING CHAMBER — The place where the fuel is burned in an engine. 29

GAS — A form of matter that has no shape of its own. A gas will contract to fill a small container or expand to fill a large container. 8

ORBIT — The path of a satellite as it circles the earth or other planet. 42

SATELLITE — A small, man-made planet which circles the earth, sun, or another planet in an orbit. 39

REACTION — Anything that happens because of another action or happening. The moving of the raft caused by the boy's jumping is a reaction. 5

VELOCITY OF ESCAPE — The speed at which a rocket must travel in order to break away from the gravity of the earth or any other planet. 40